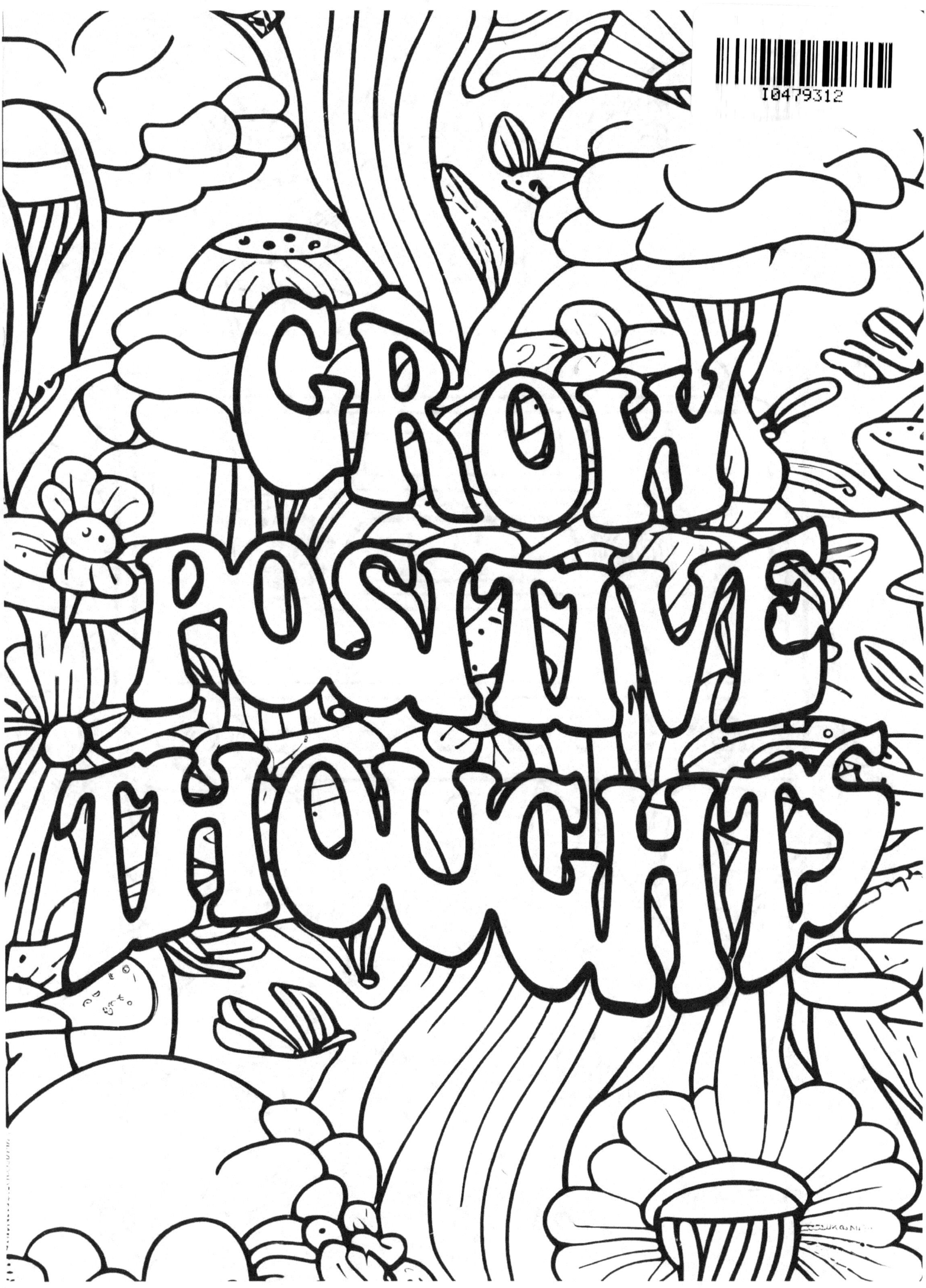
GROW
POSITIVE
THOUGHTS

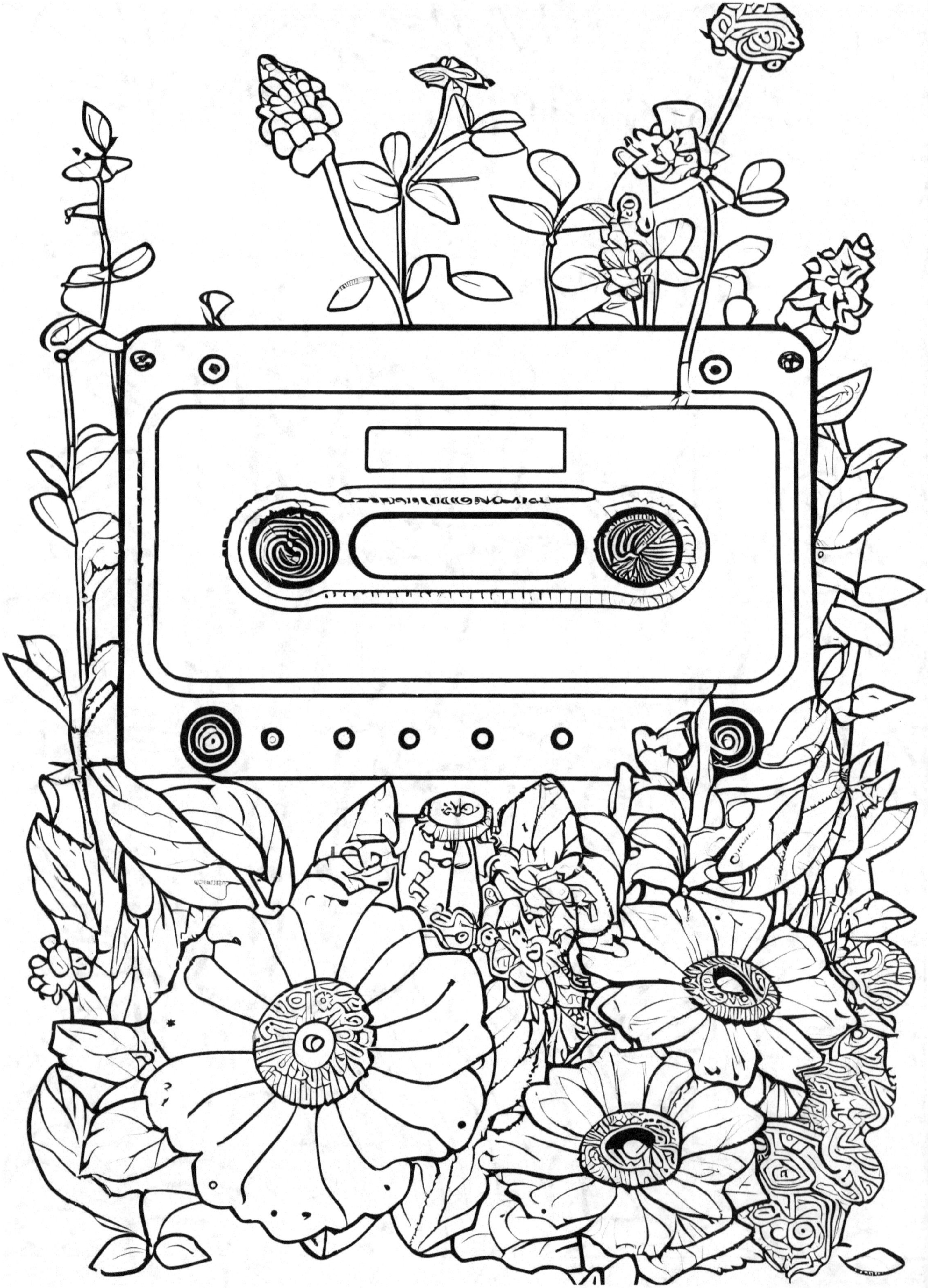

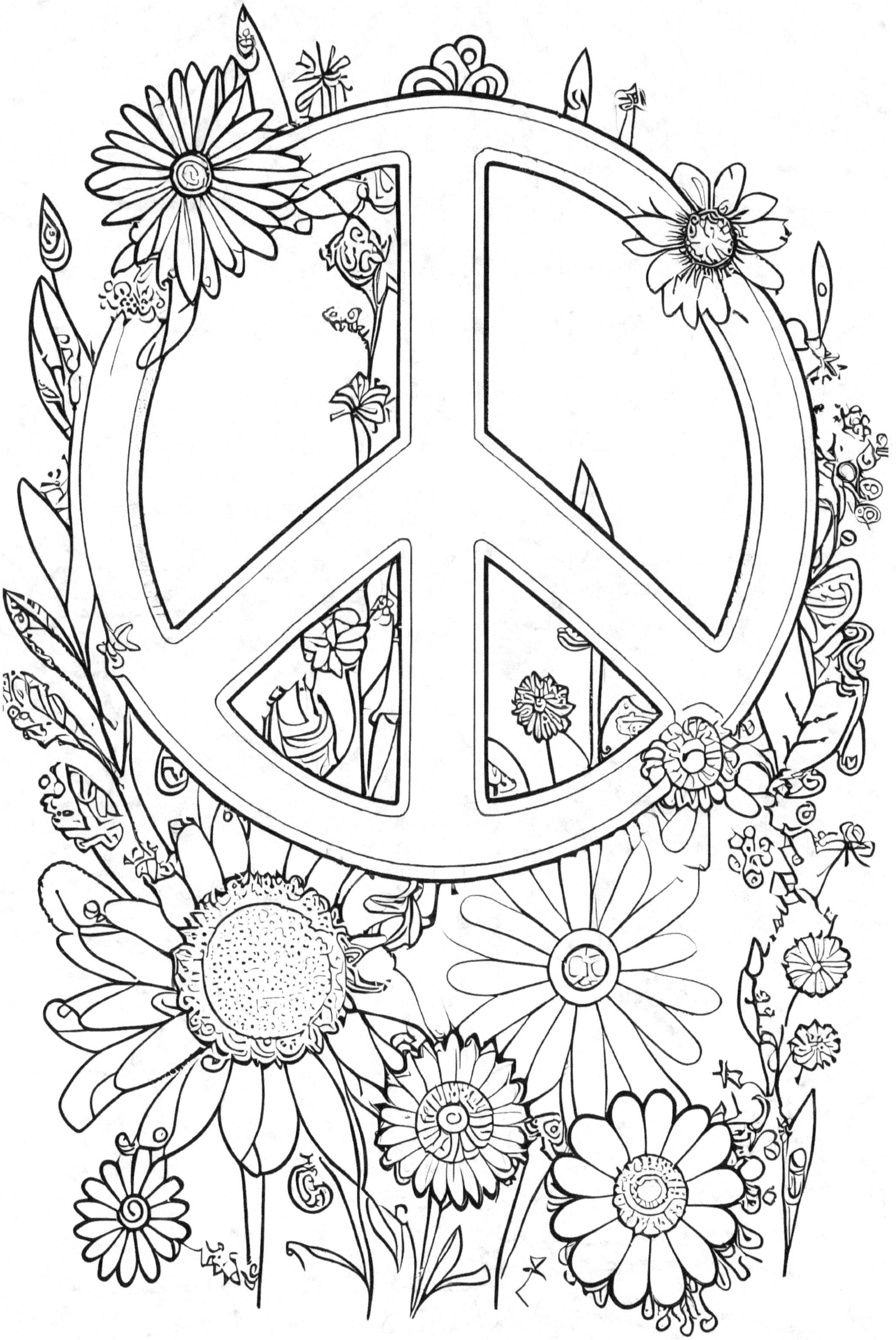

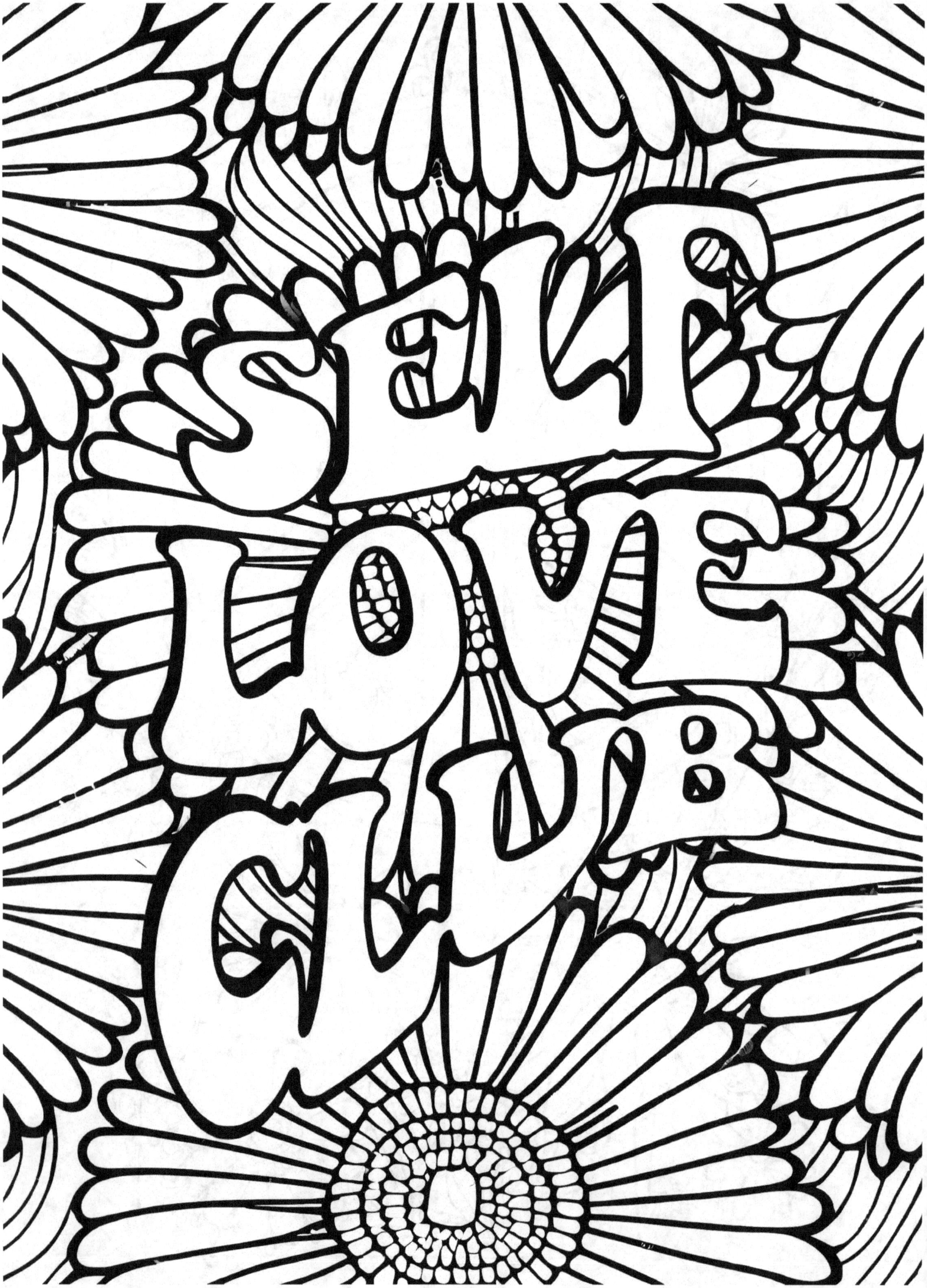
SELF
LOVE
CLUB

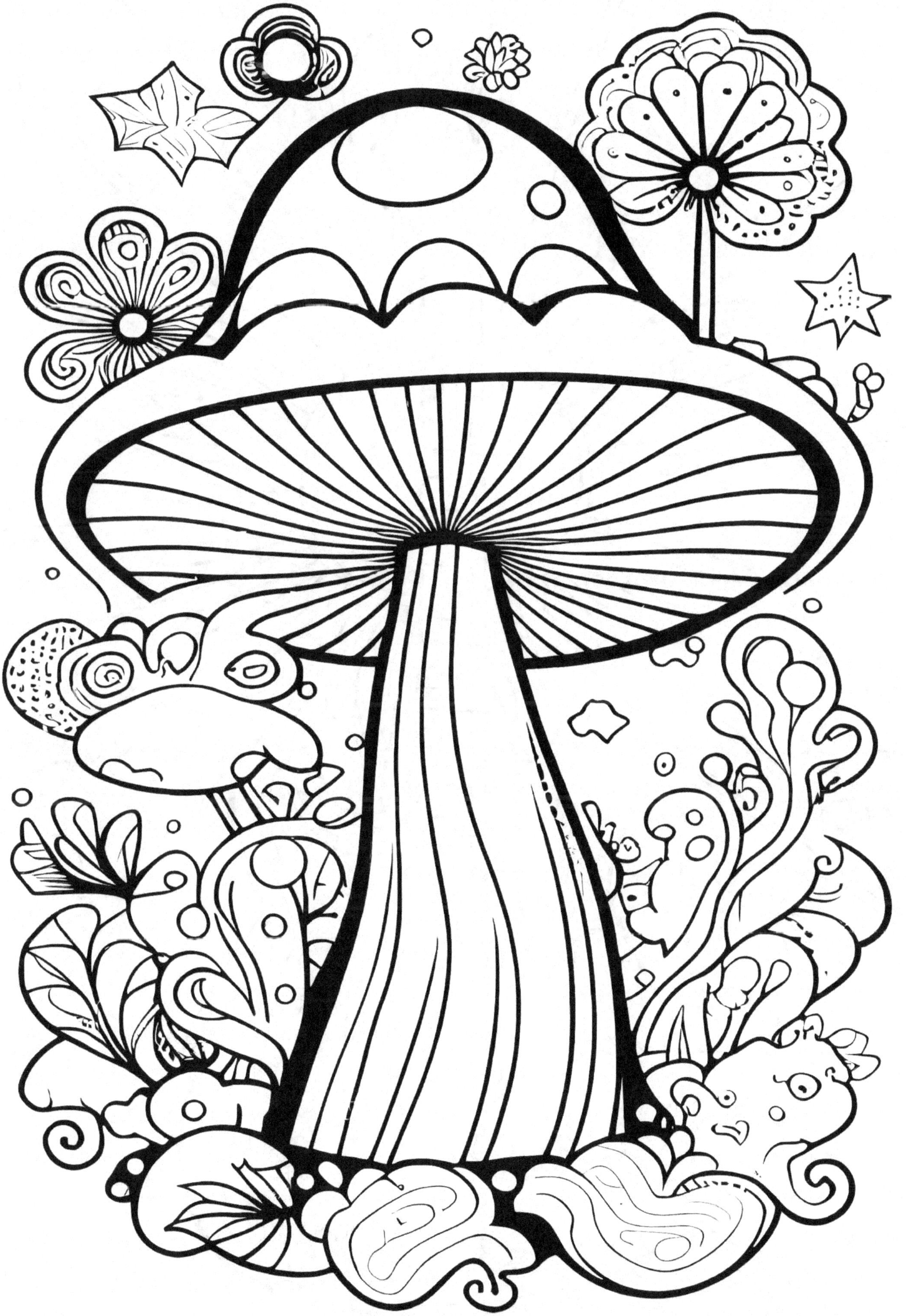

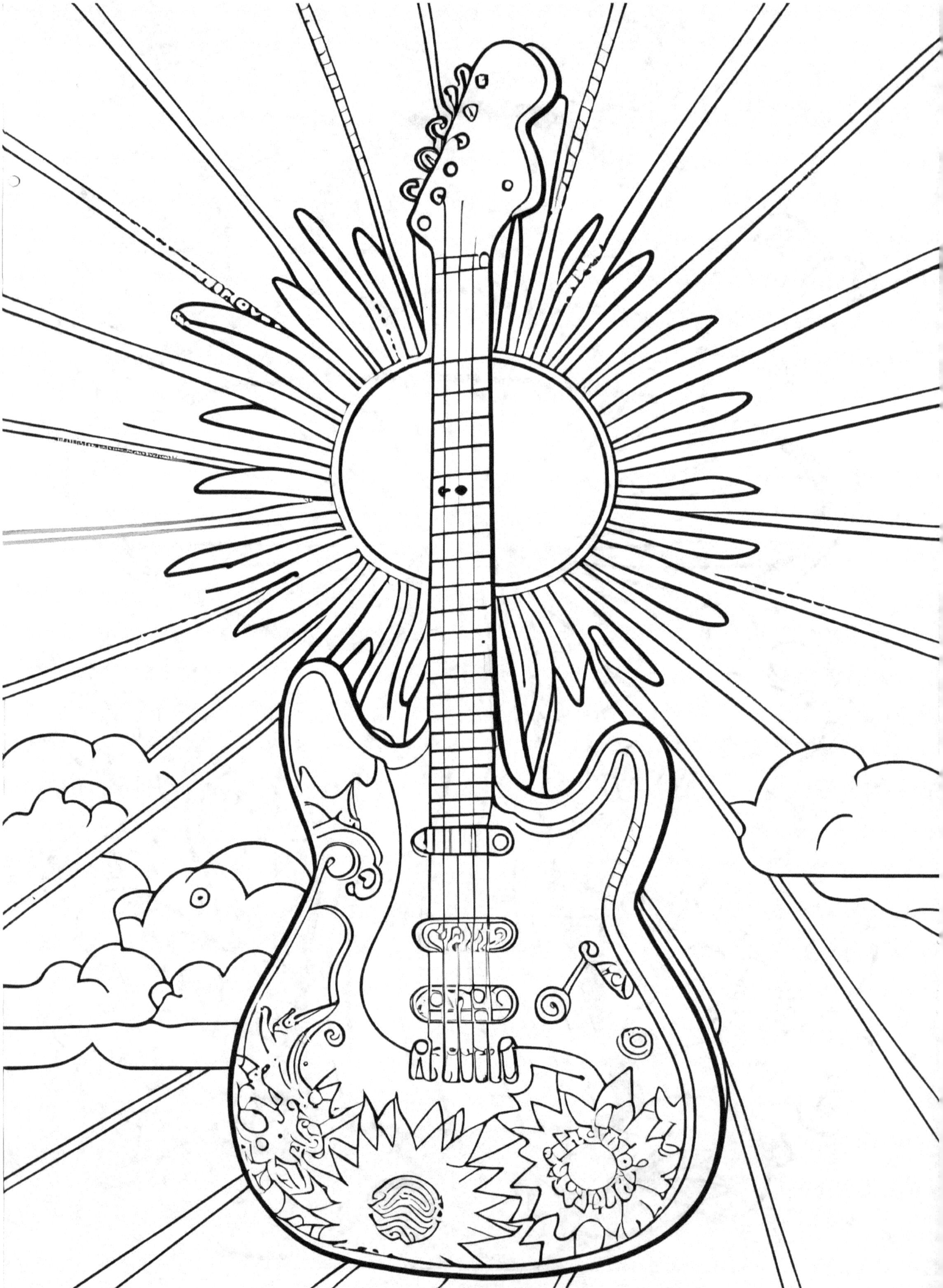

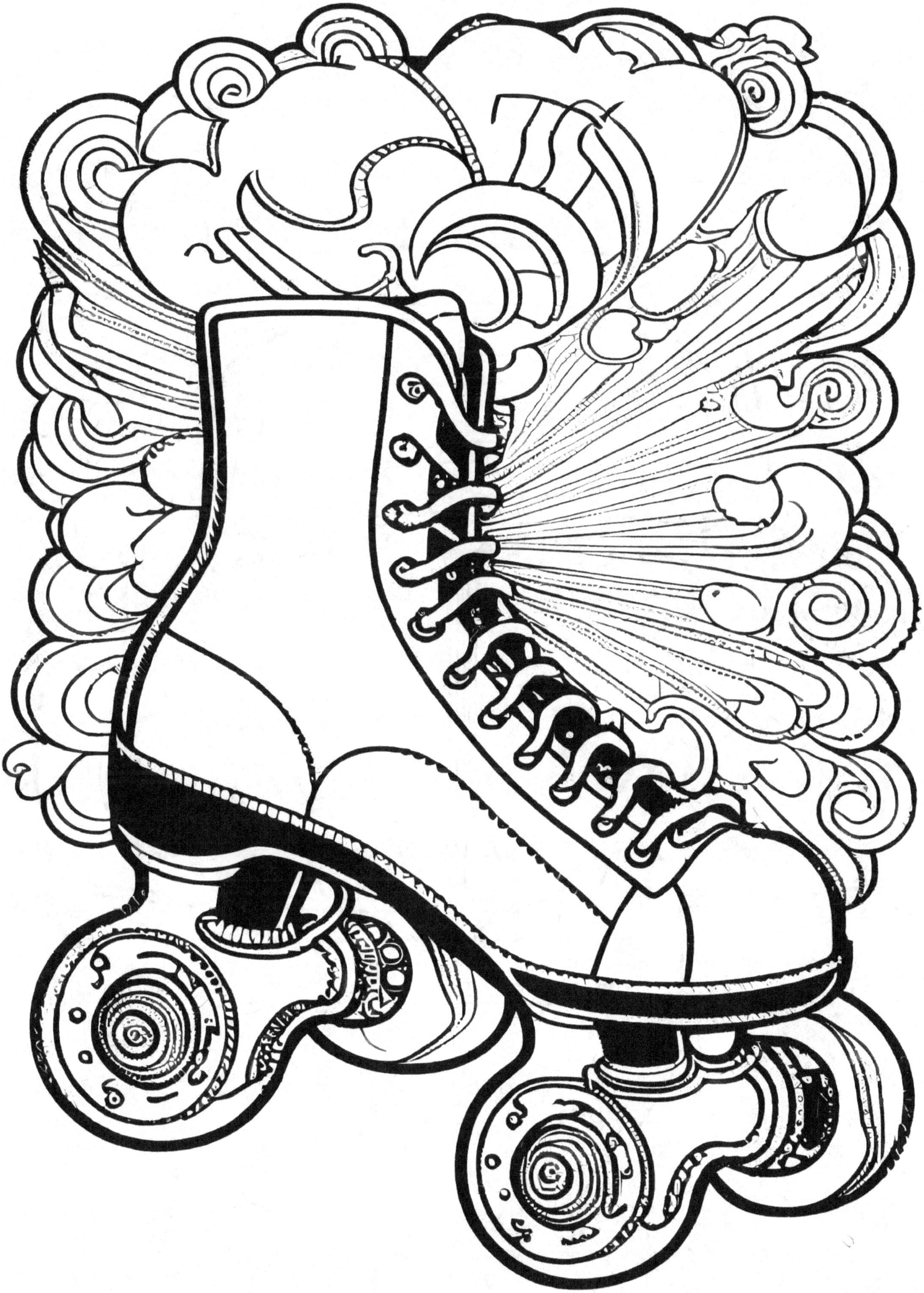

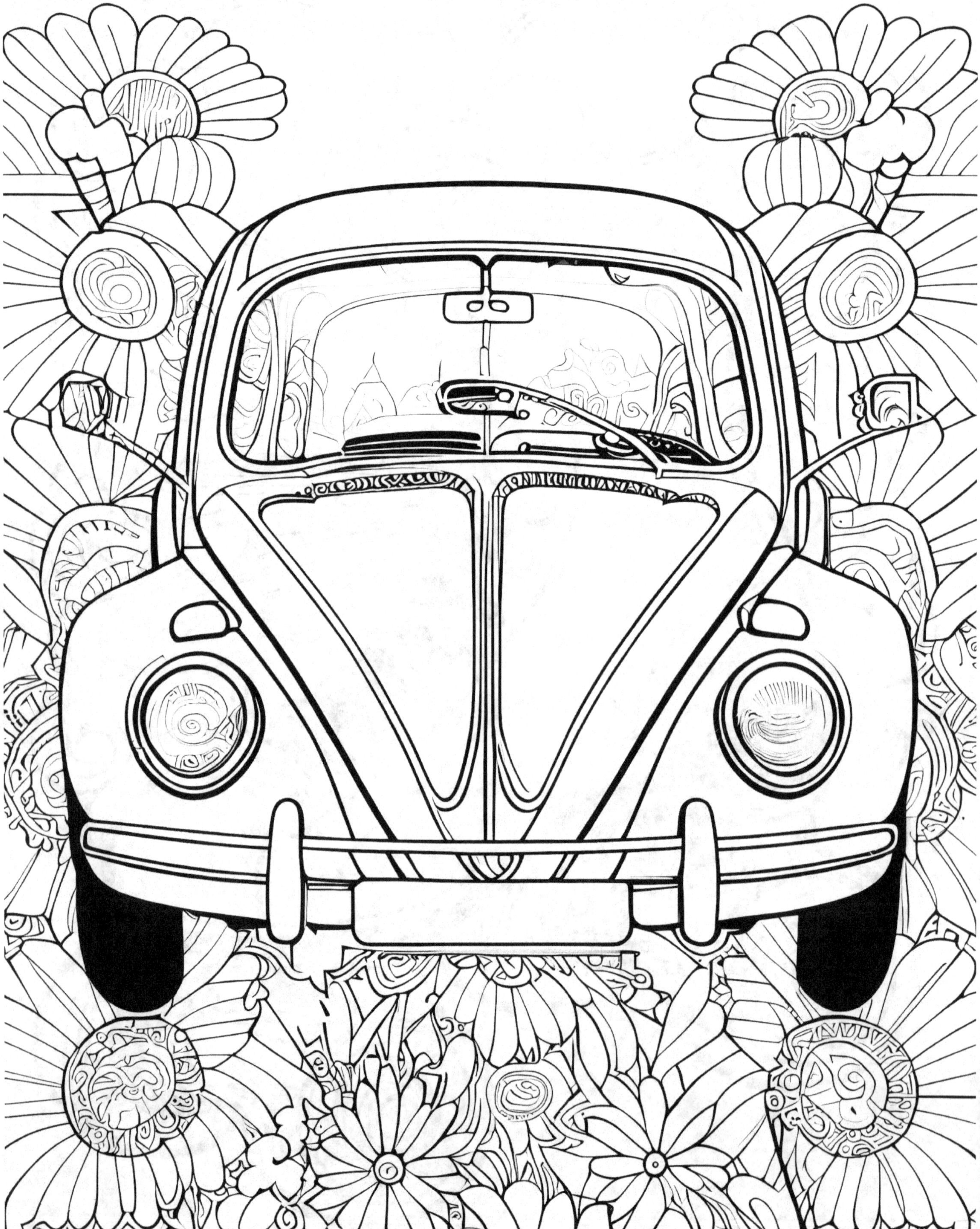

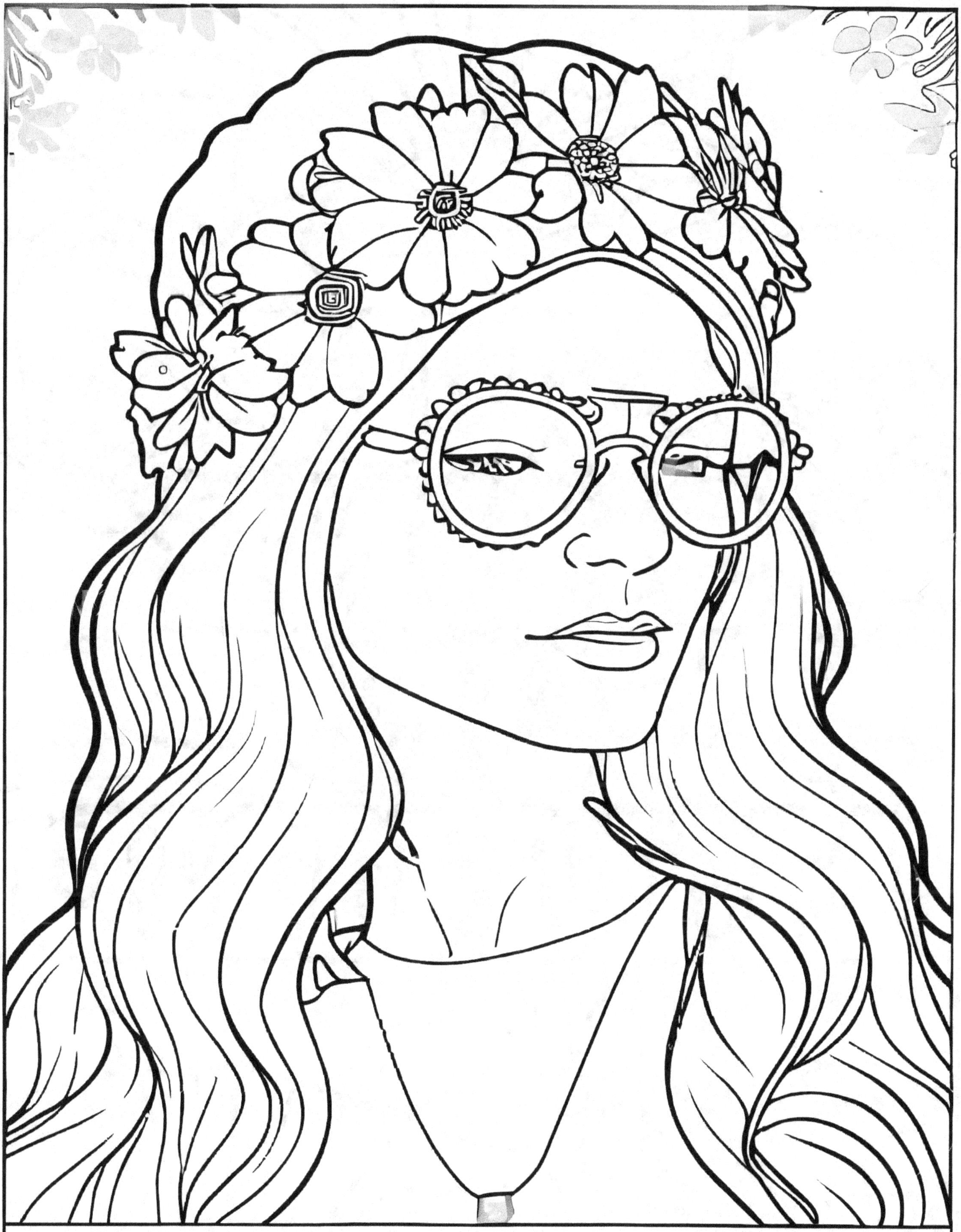

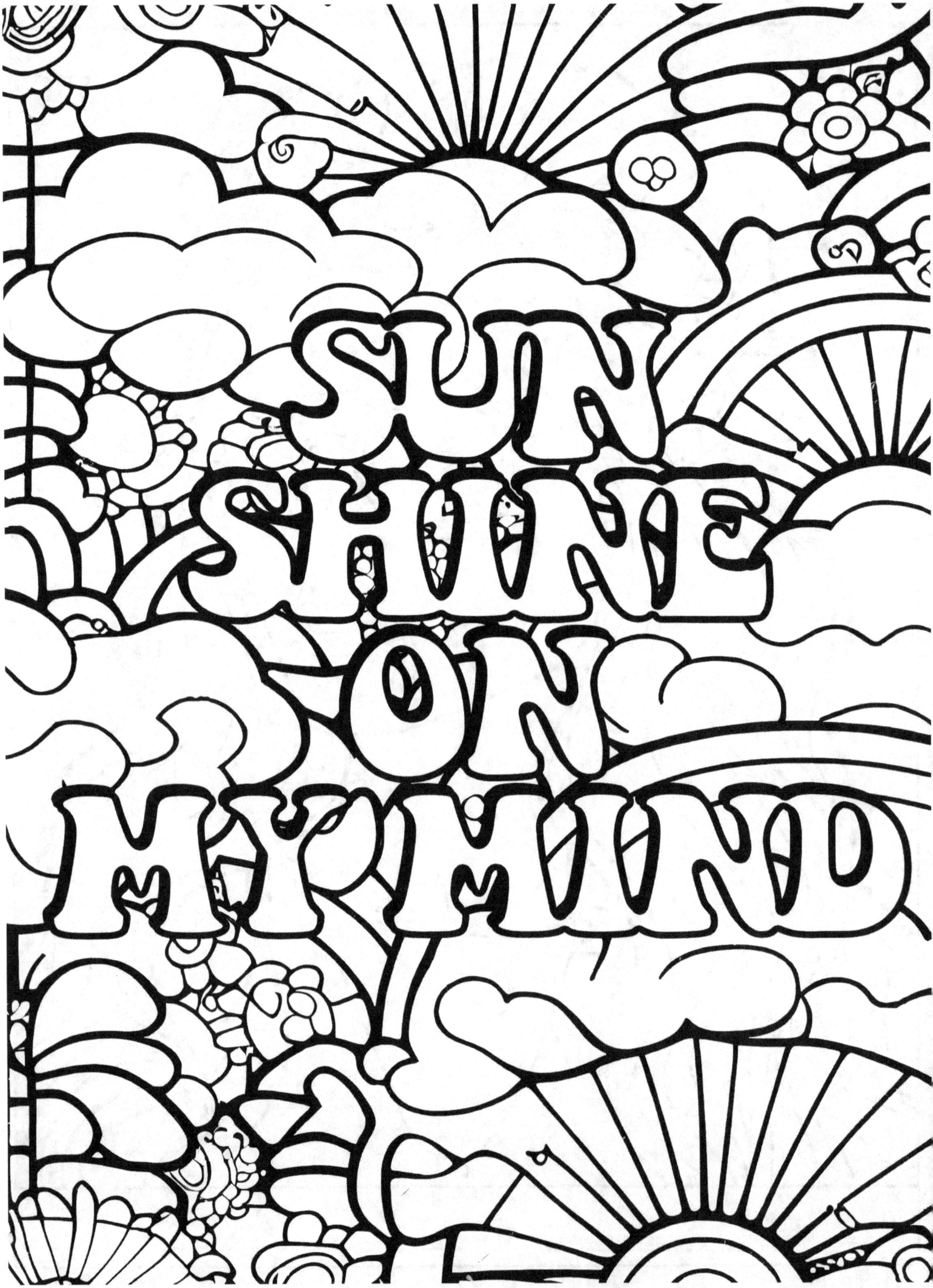
SUN
SHINE
ON
MY MIND

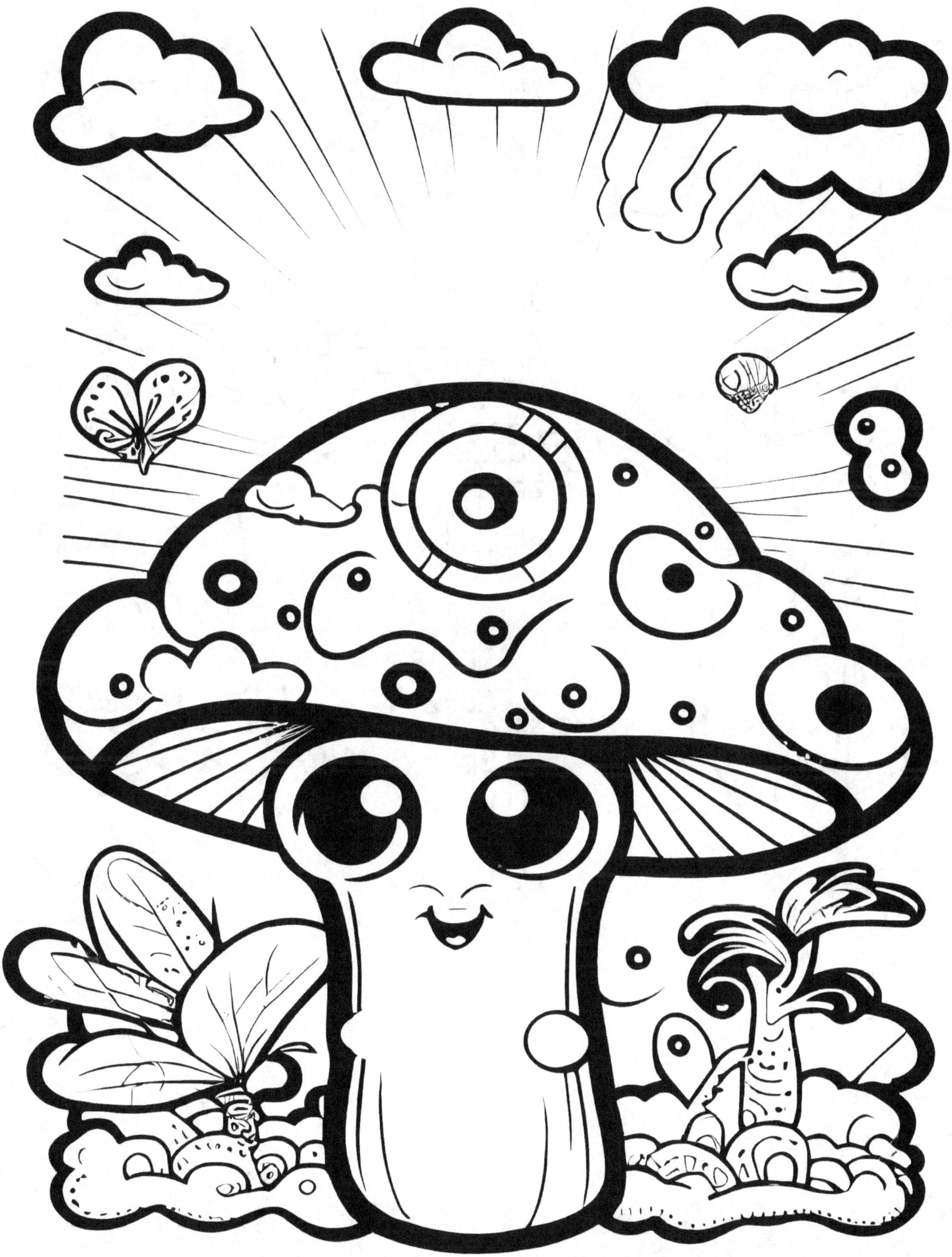

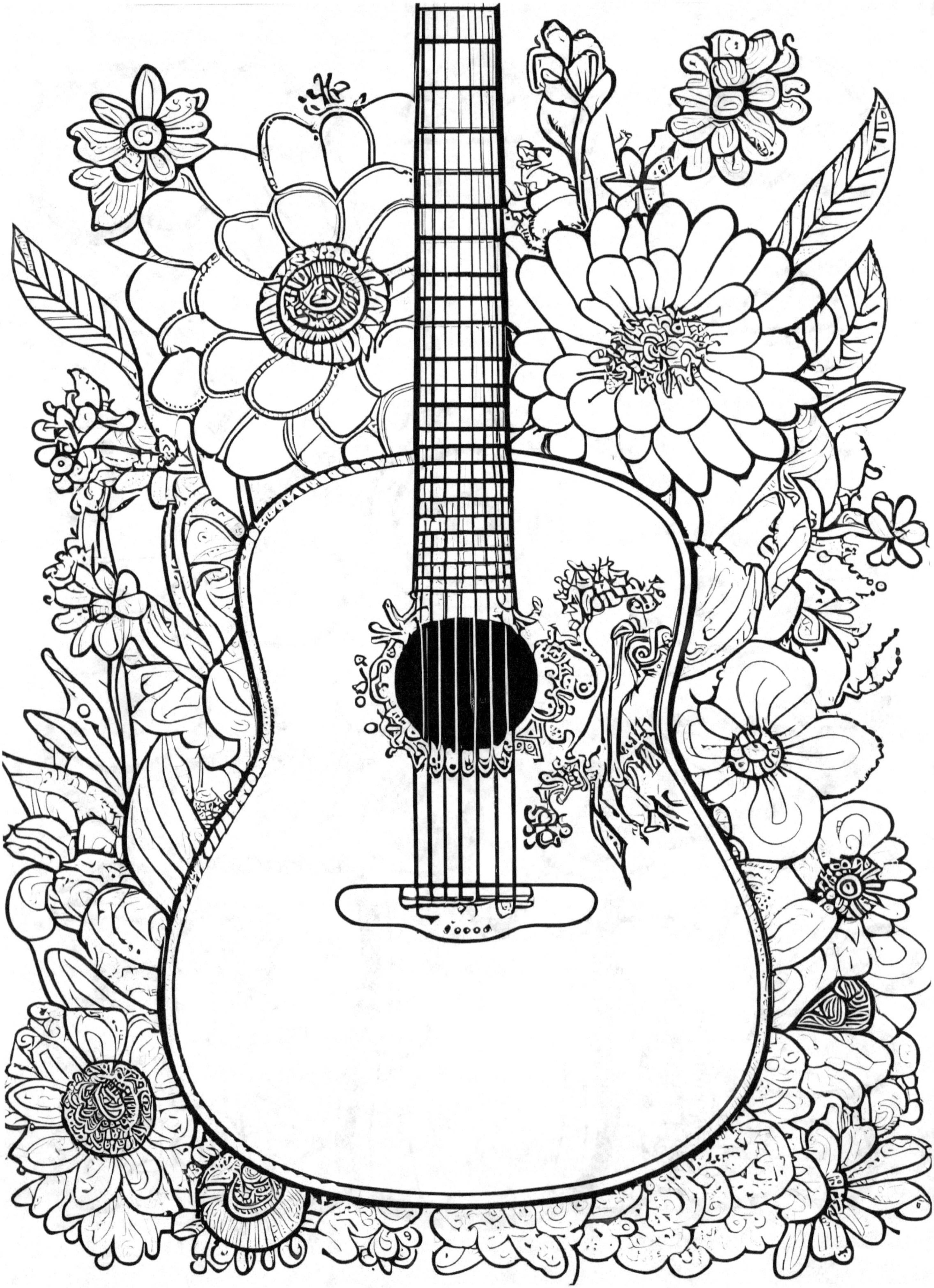

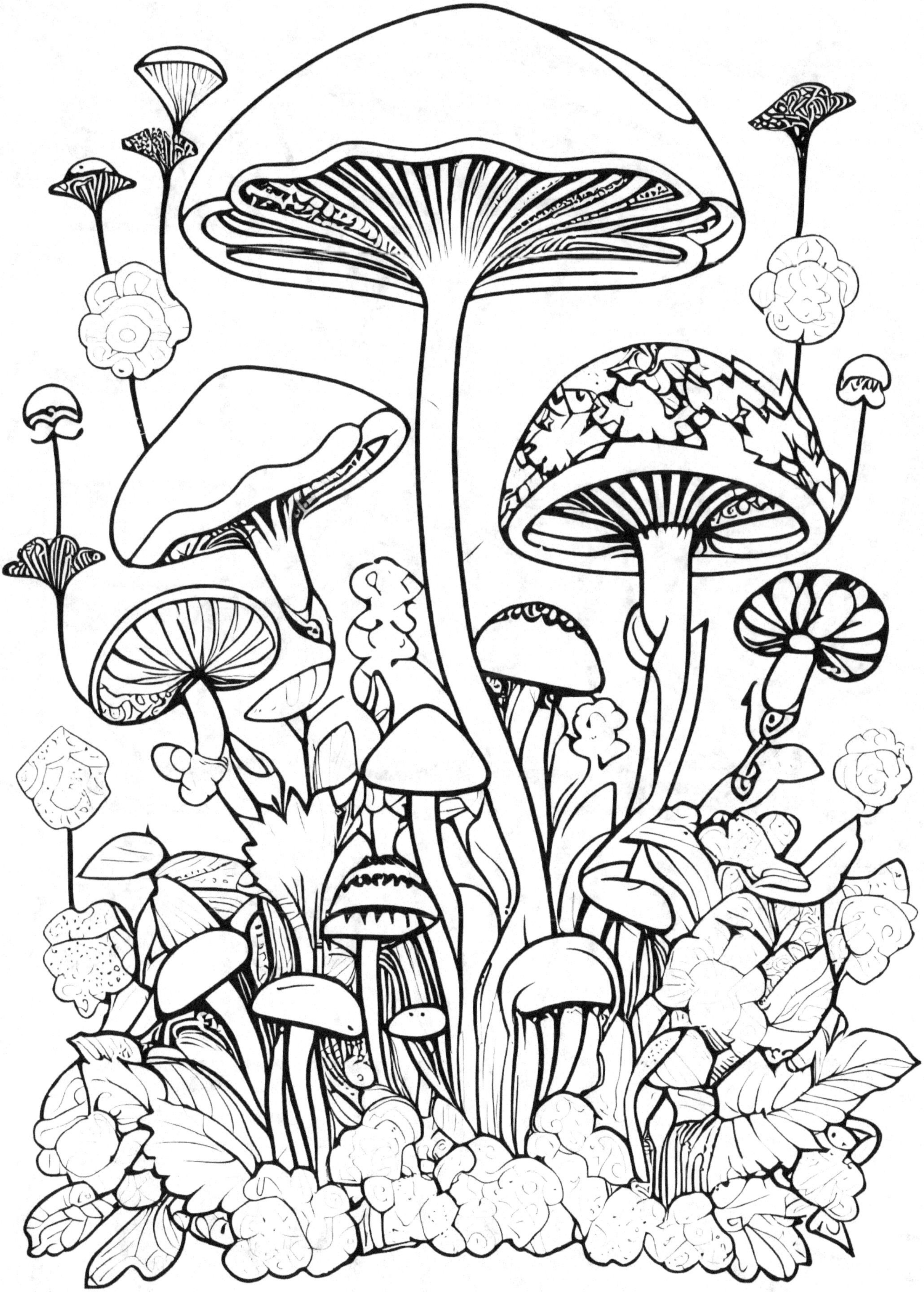

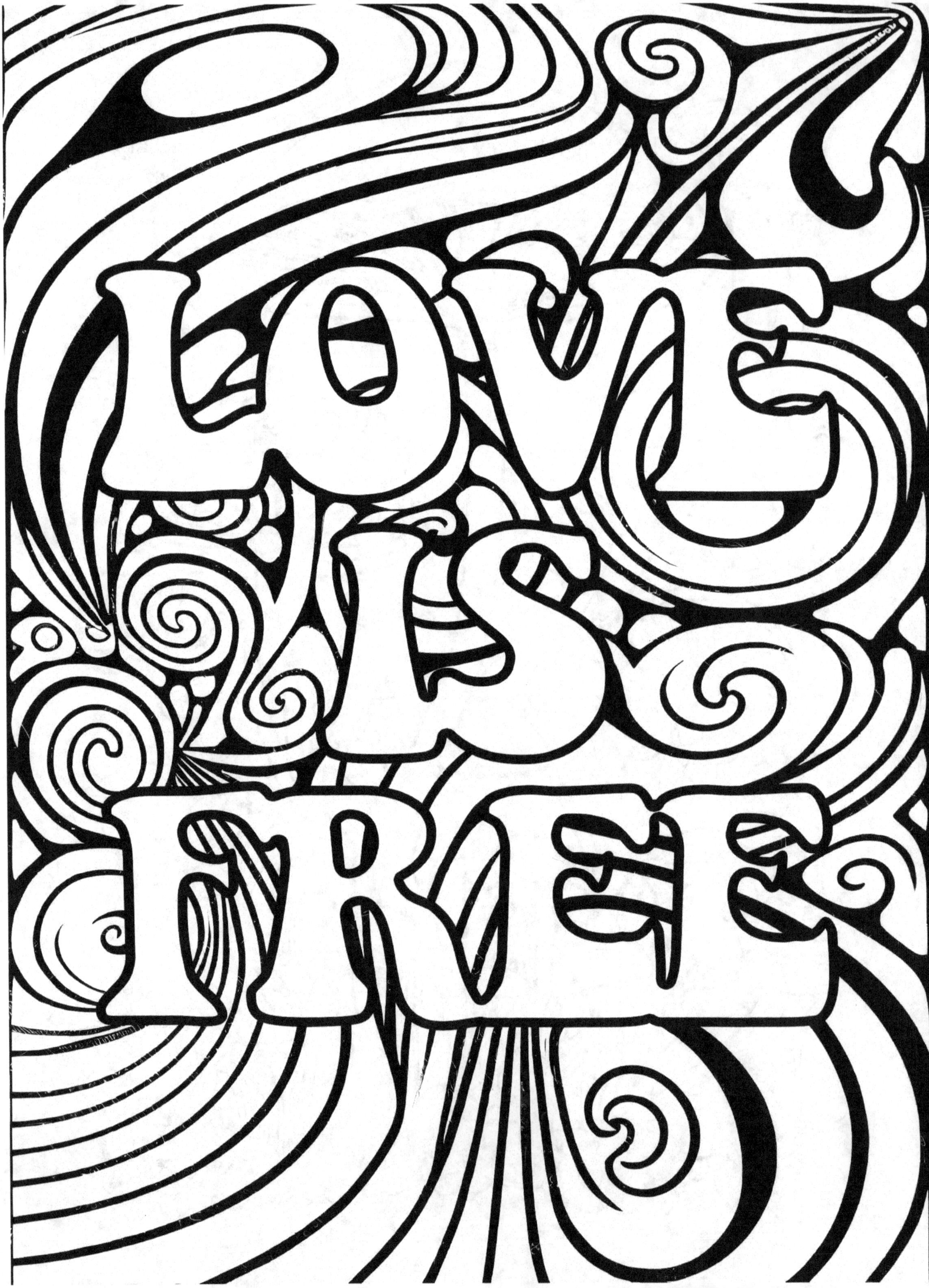
LOVE
IS
FREE

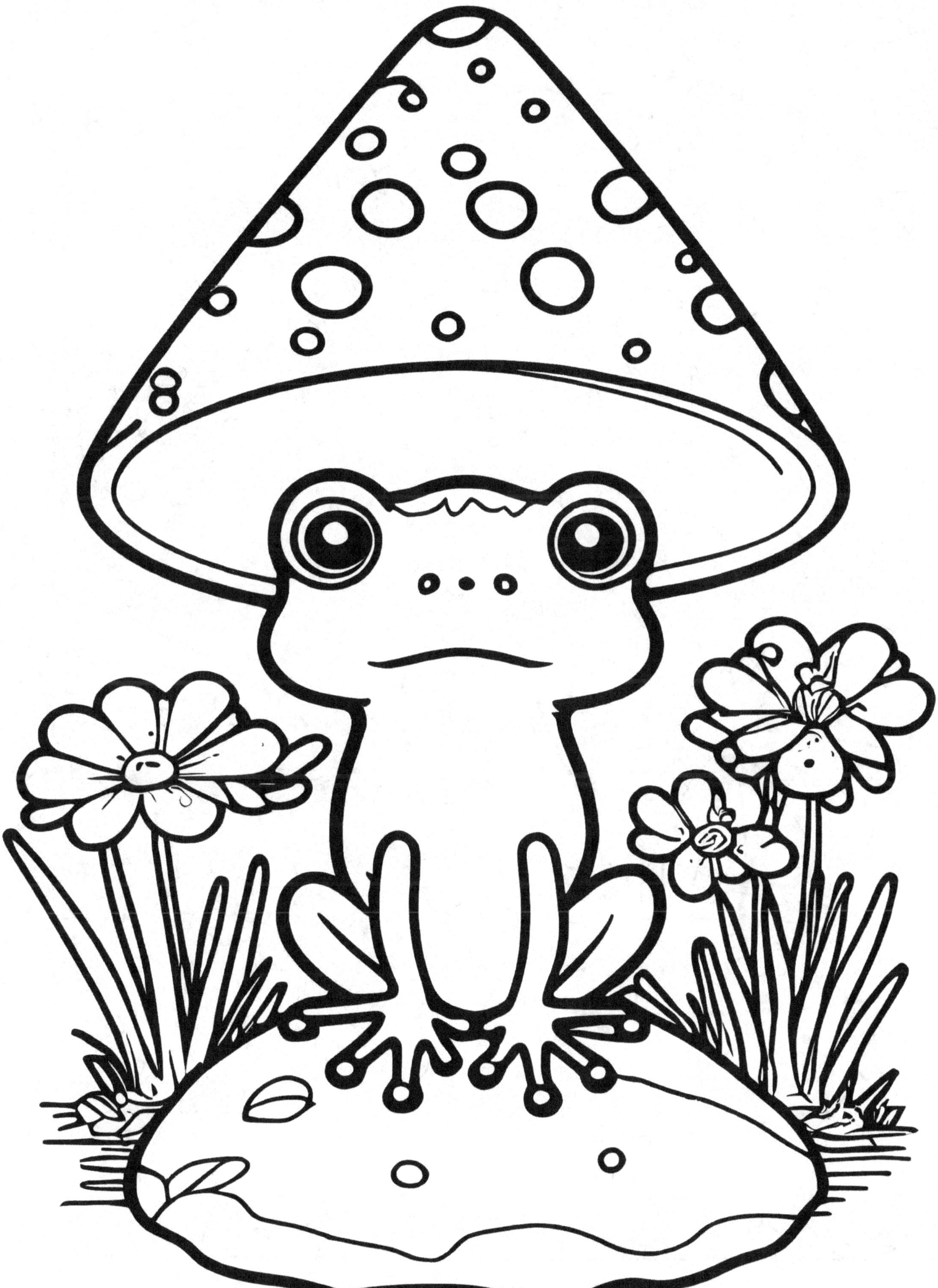

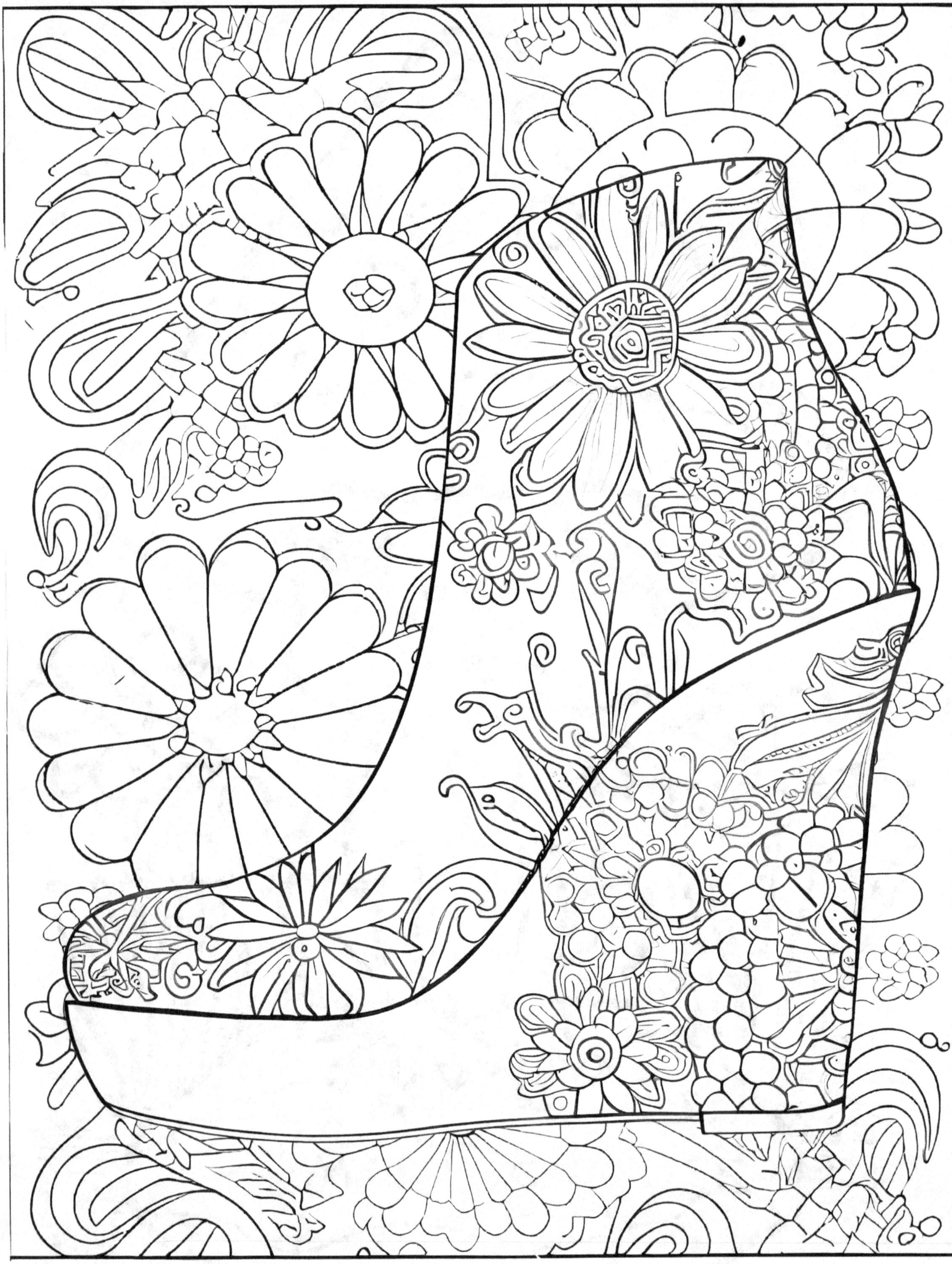

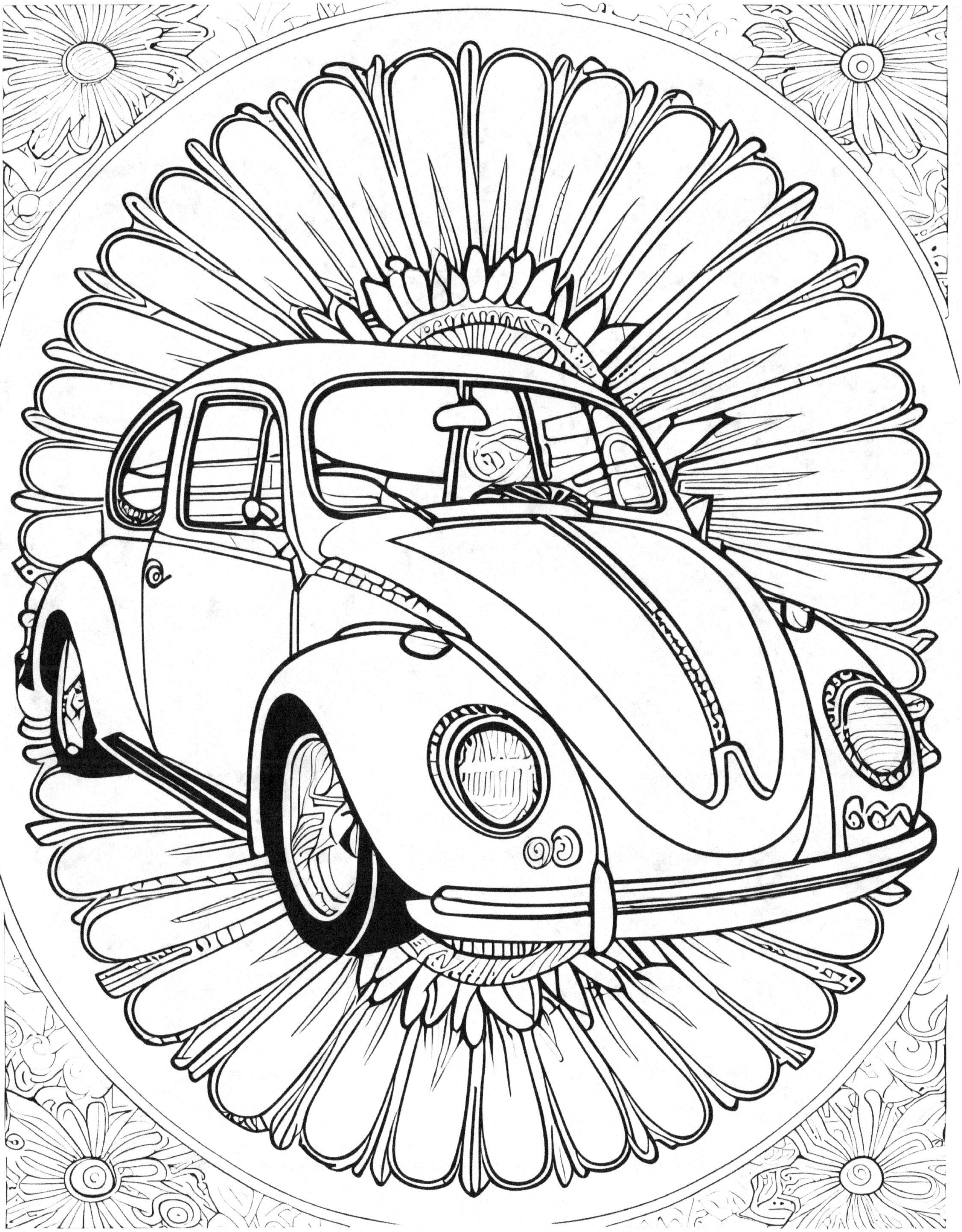

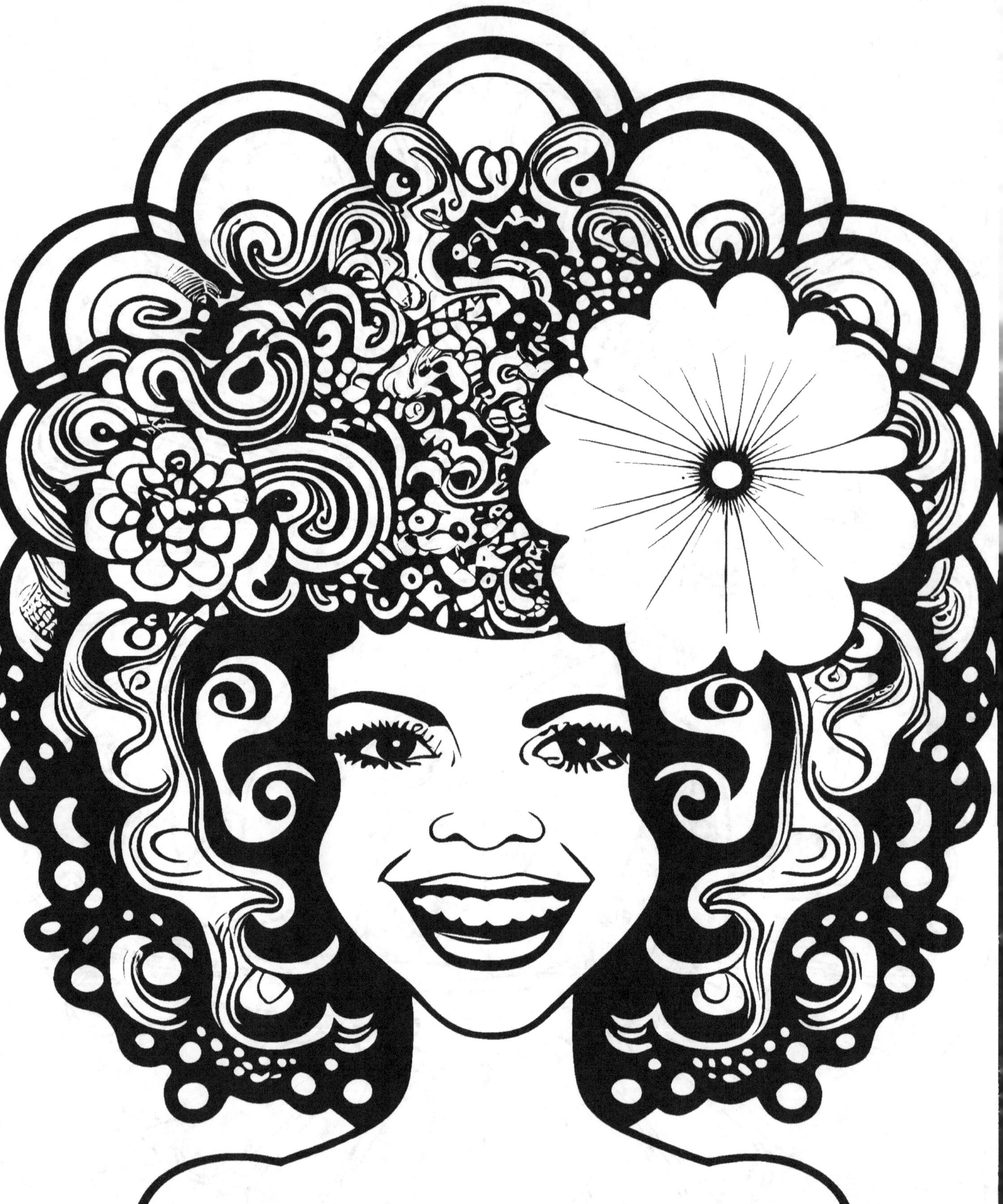

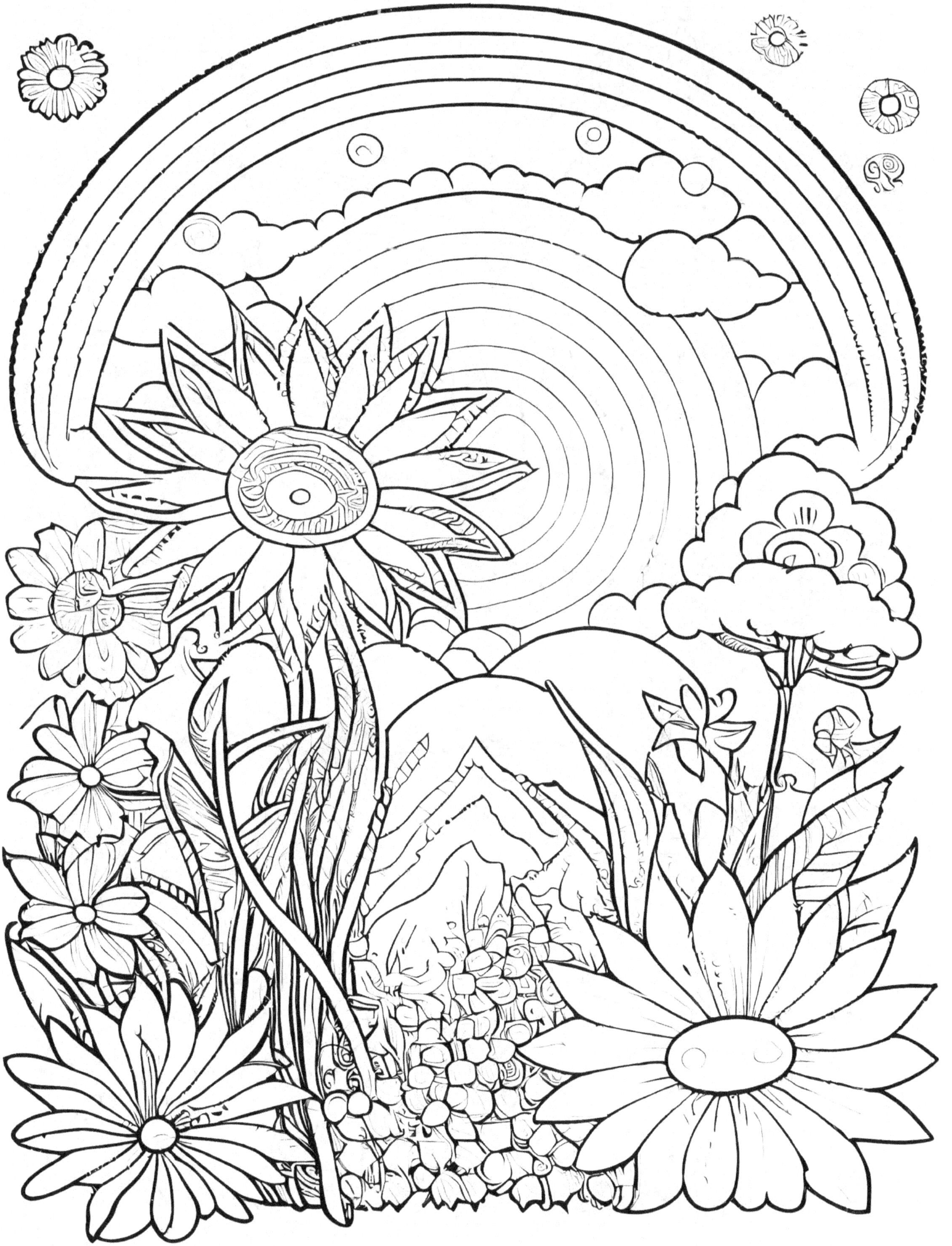

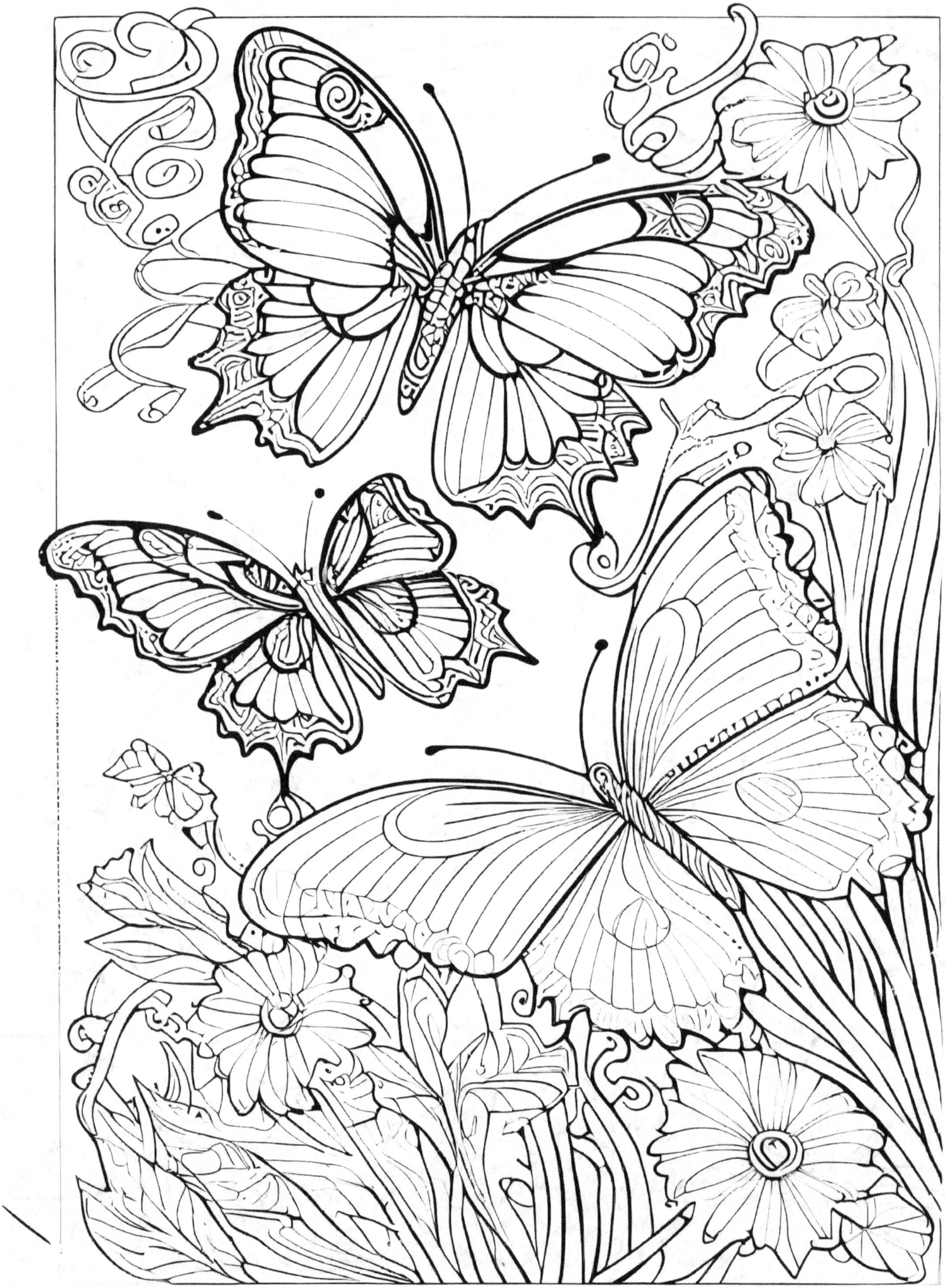

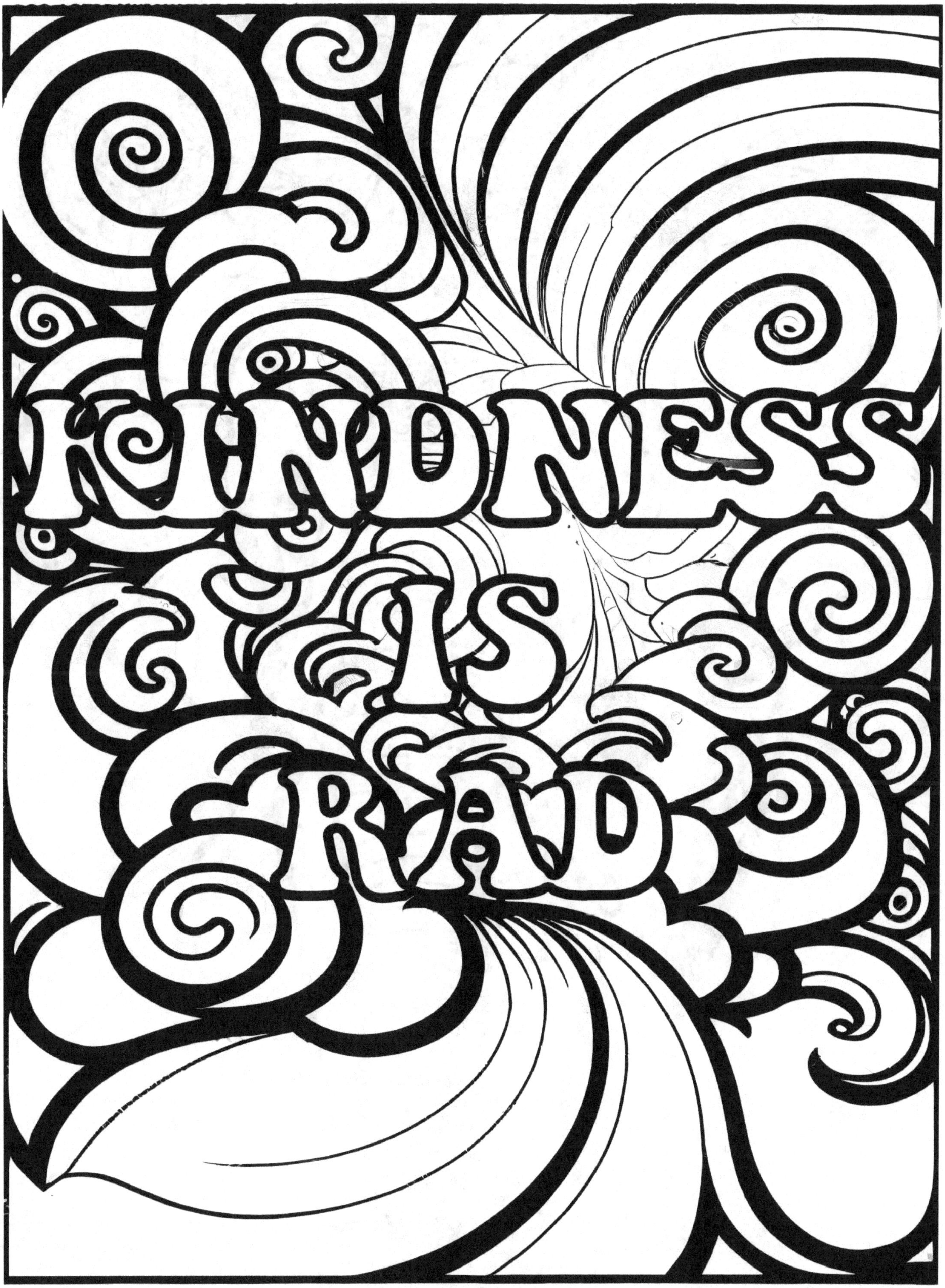
KINDNESS
IS
RAD

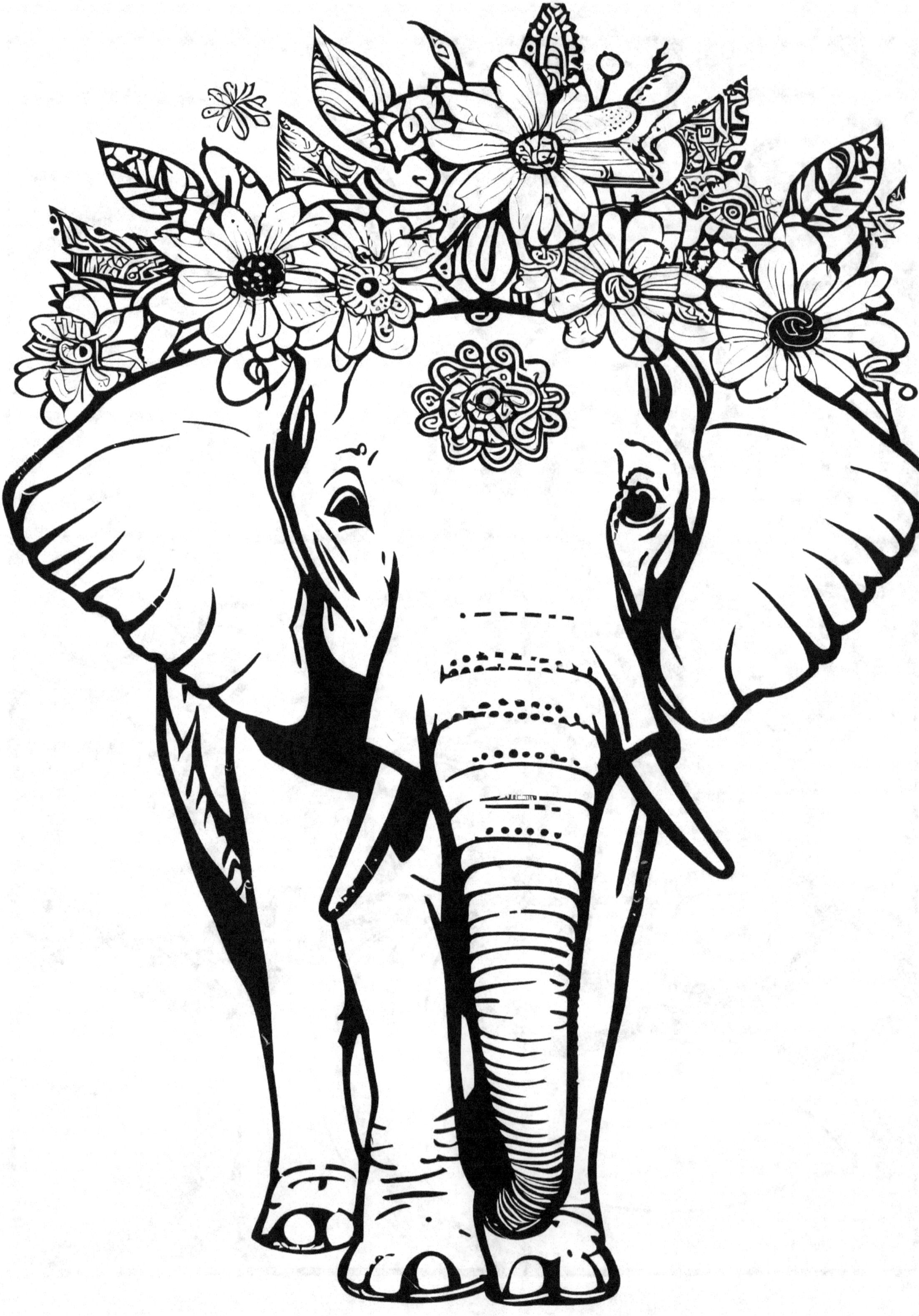

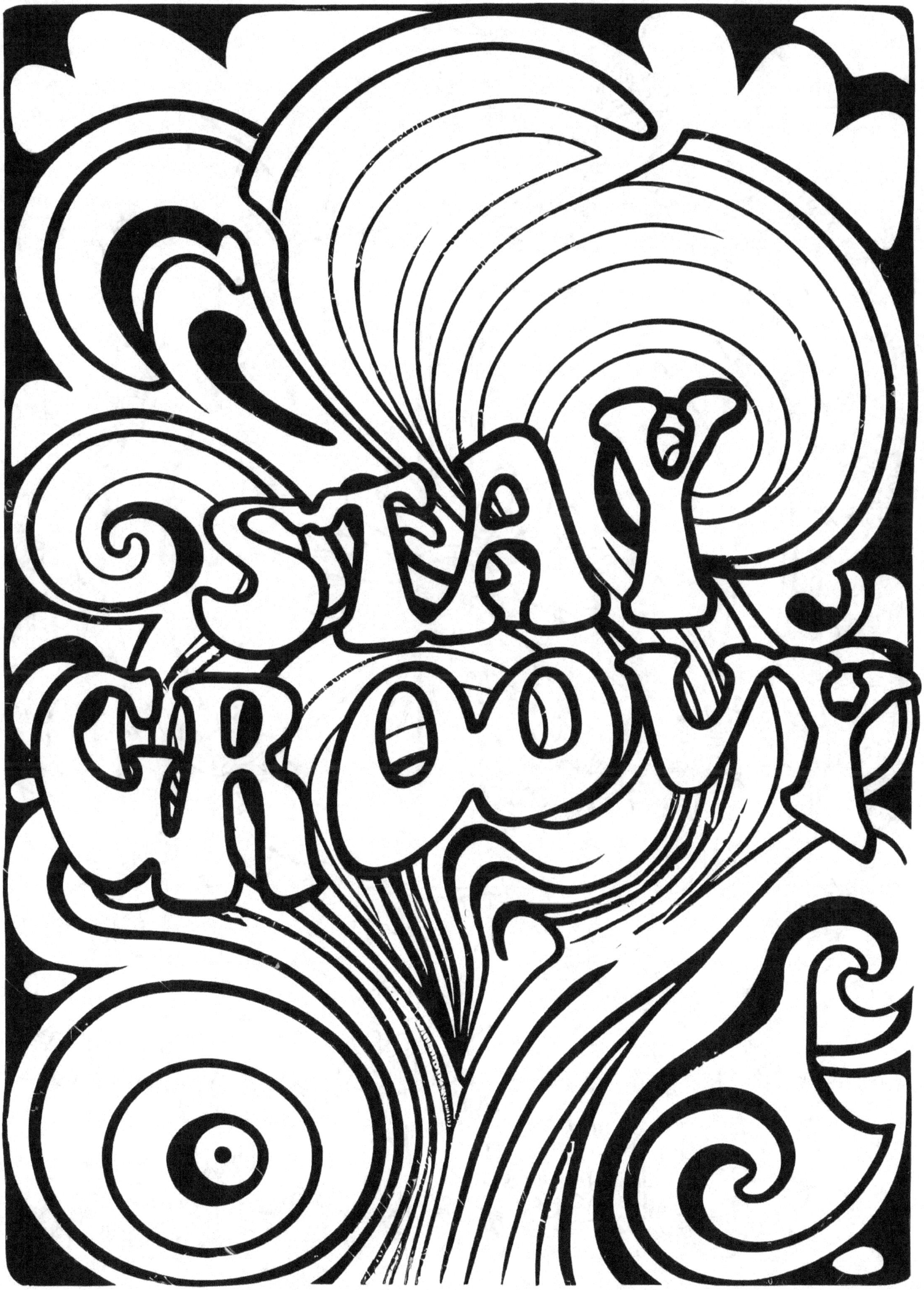
STAY GROOVY

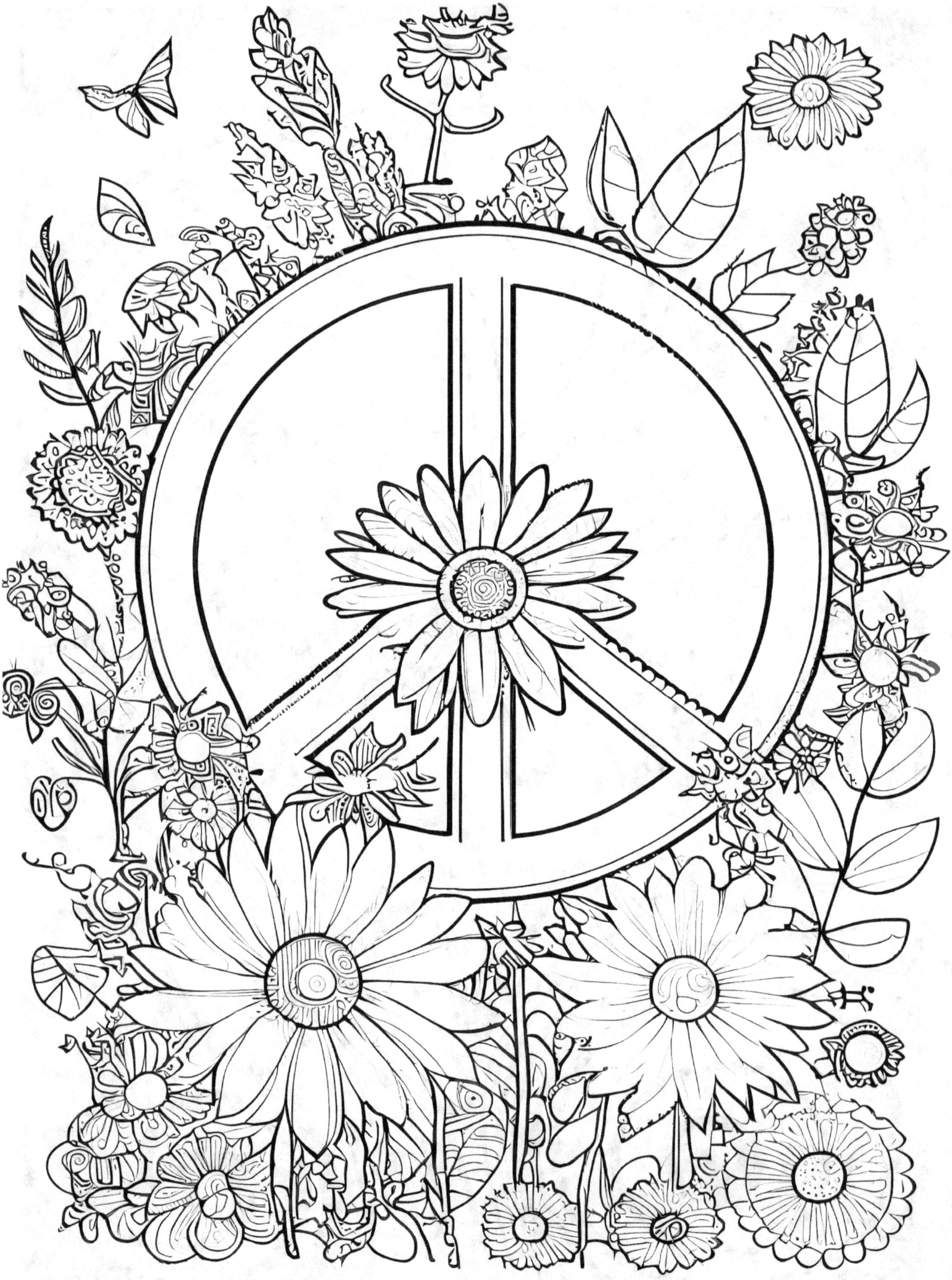

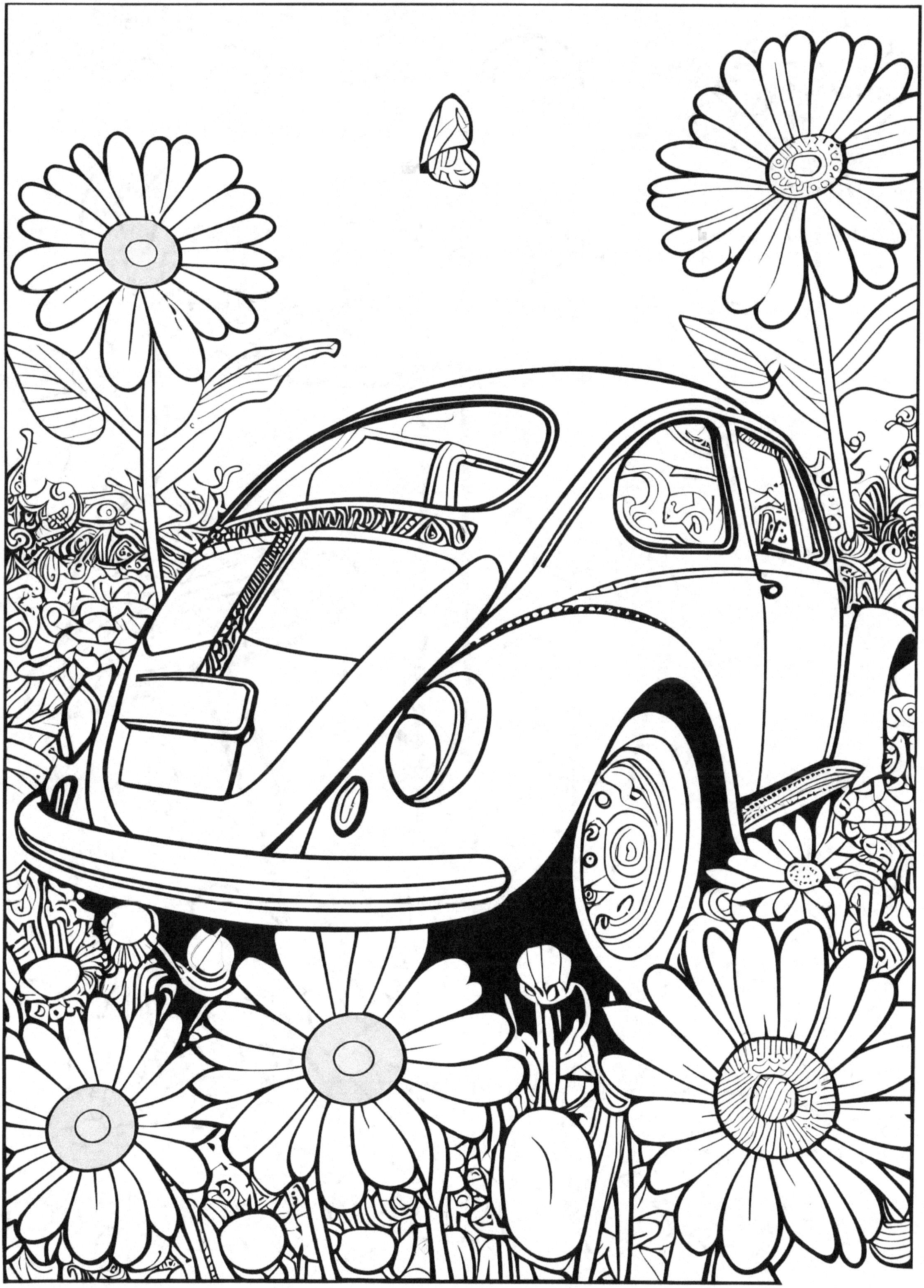

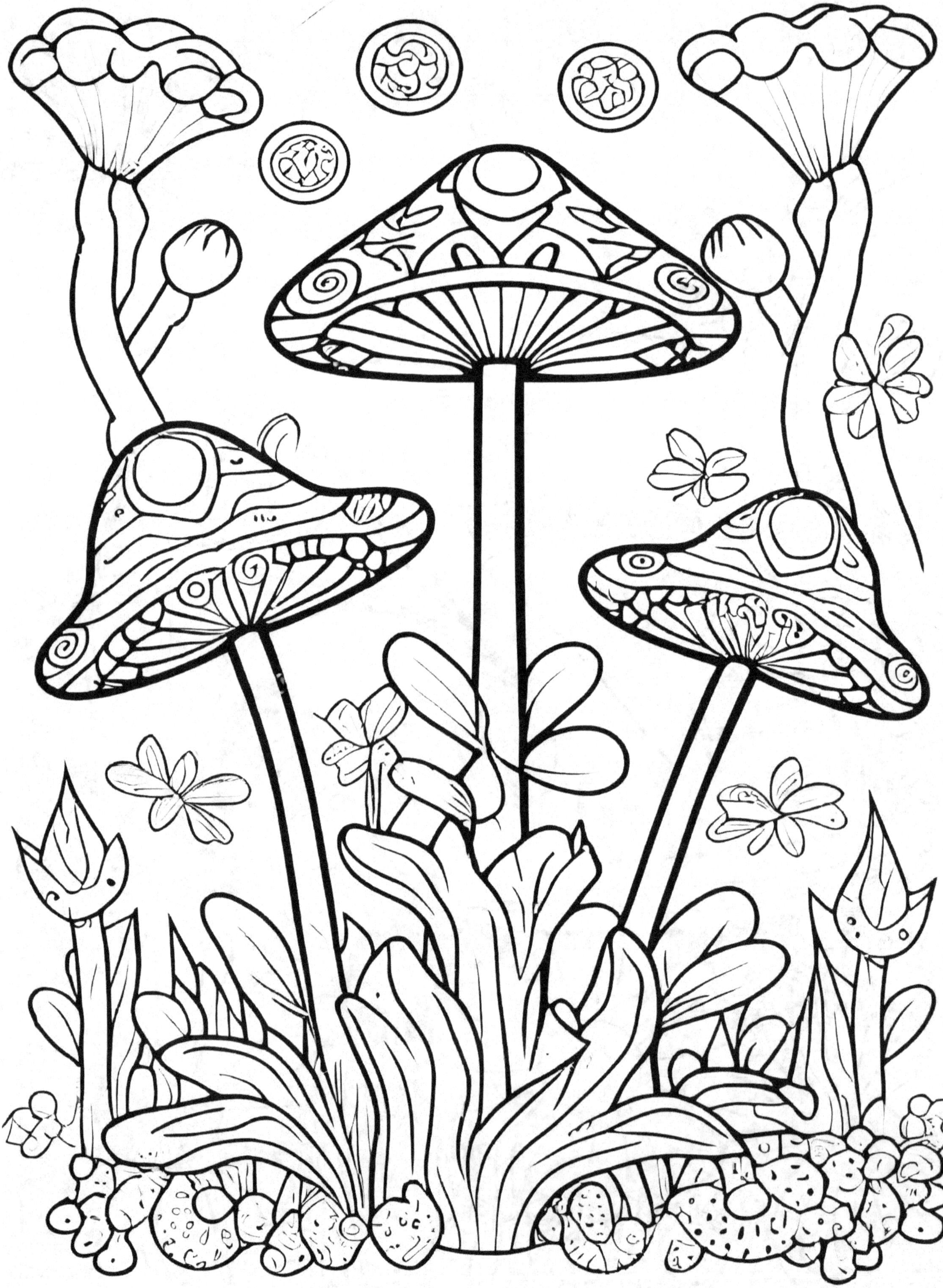

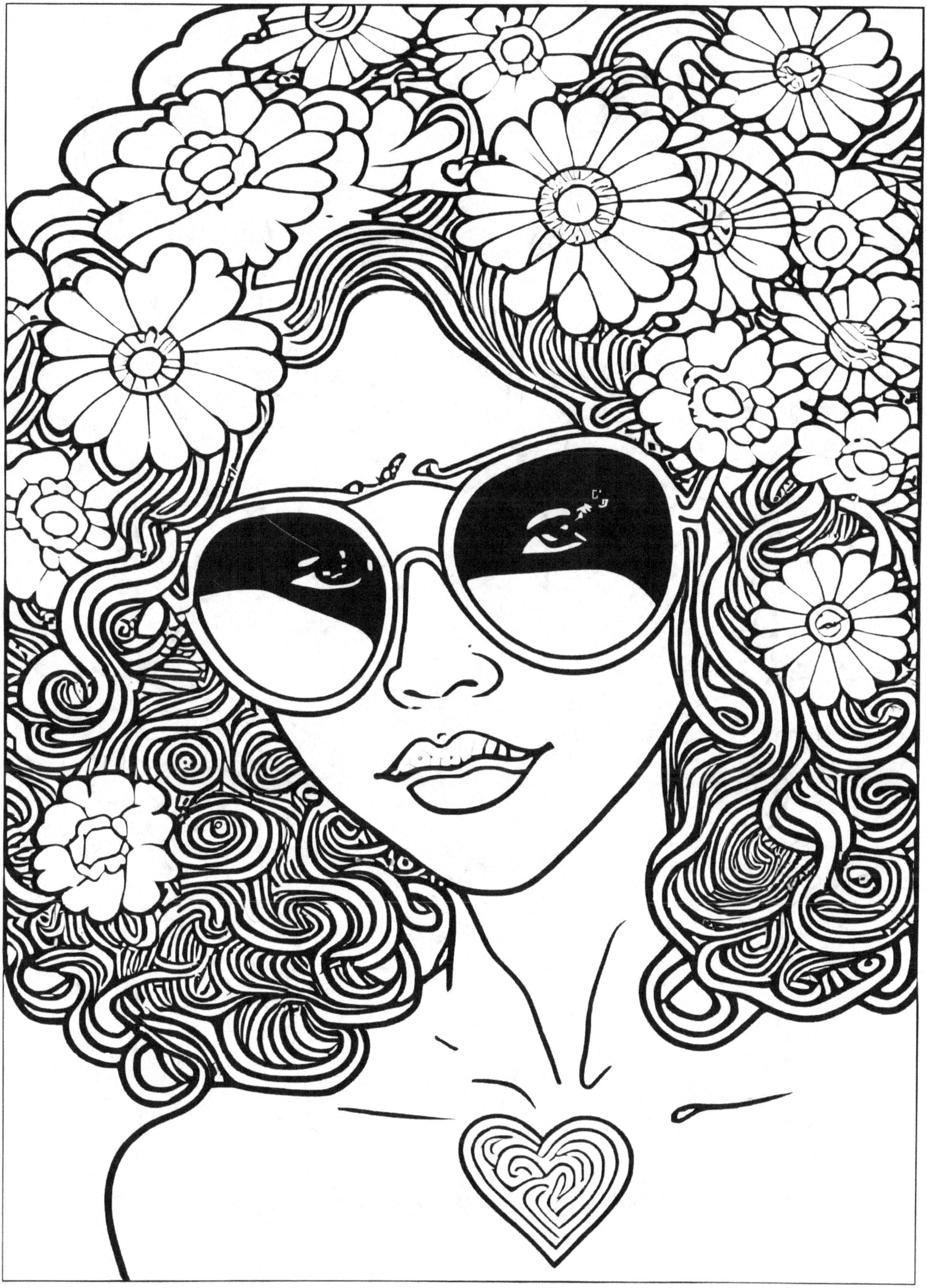

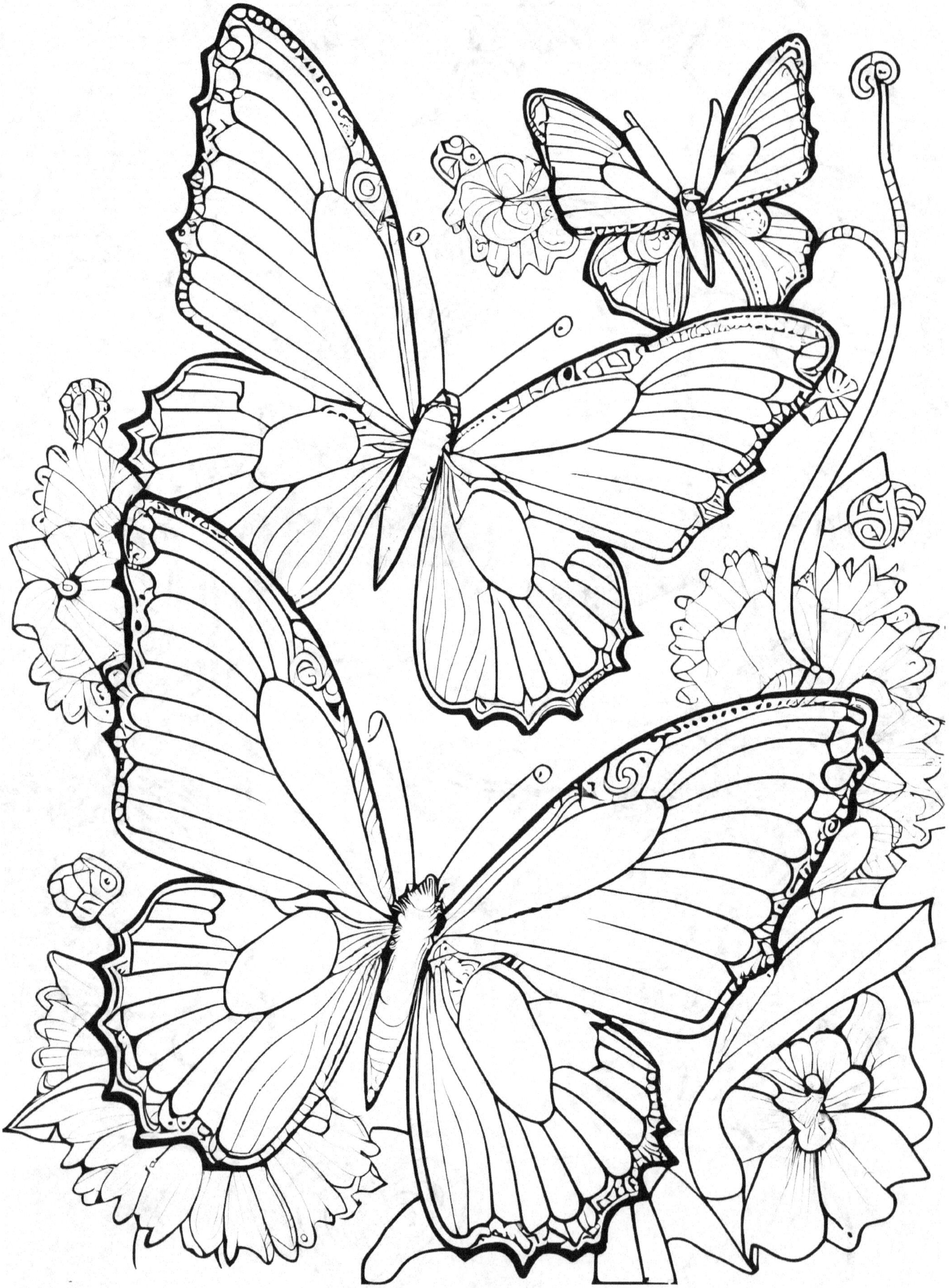

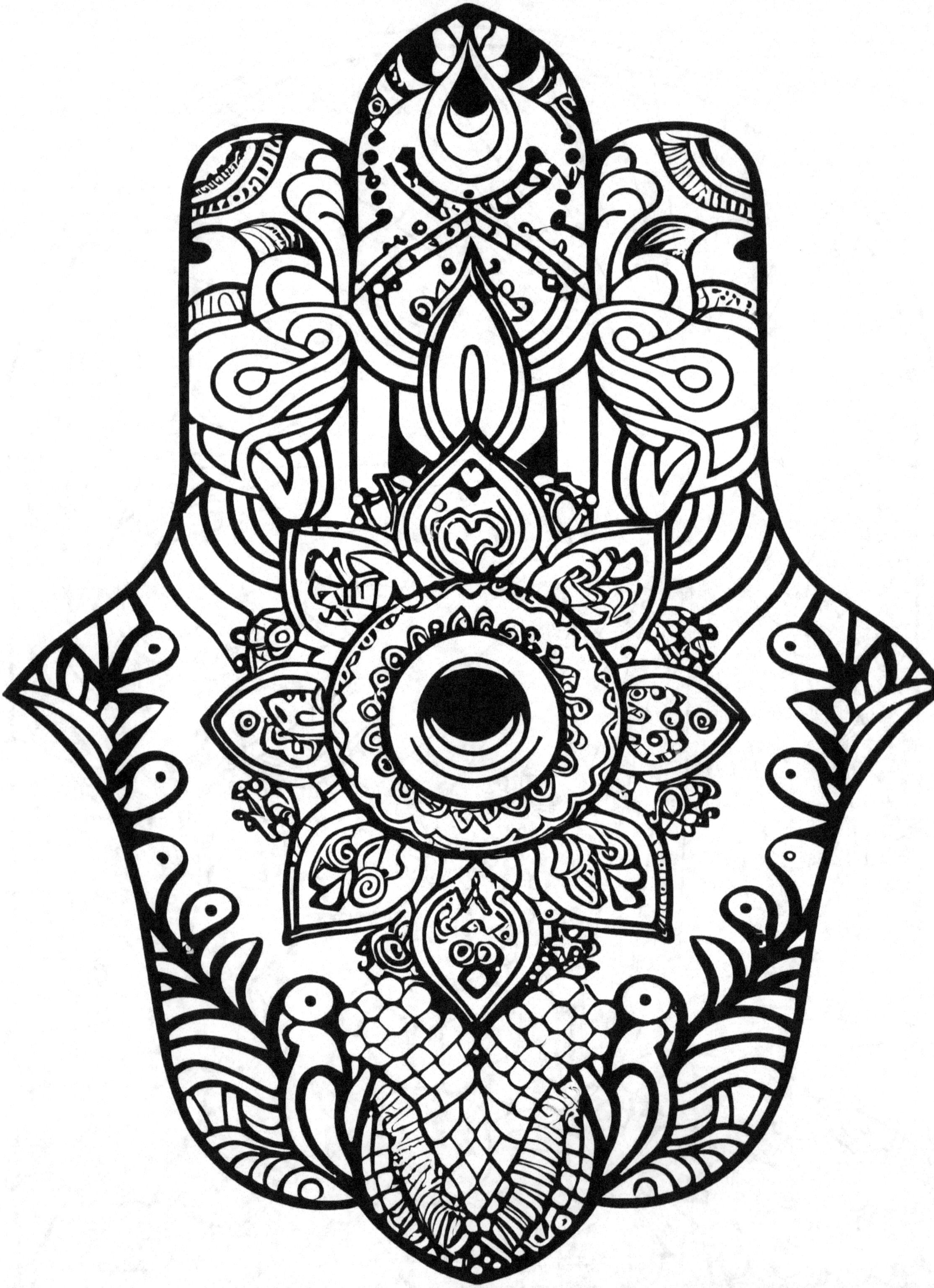

www.ingramcontent.com/pod-product-compliance
Lightning Source LLC
Chambersburg PA
CBHW081712220526
45467CB00028B/2791
* 9 7 9 8 3 9 1 4 5 1 6 4 8 *